ZERO-BASED BUDGETING MAGIC

Transform Your Finances with Purpose and Precision

Sinéad Hoben

For my family.

Money often costs too much.

RALPH WALDO EMERSON

CONTENTS

PREFACE

As someone who has struggled with managing my finances in the past, I know firsthand how overwhelming and stressful it can be to feel like your money is controlling you instead of the other way around. But I also know that there is hope and a way forward. That's why I wrote "Zero-Based Budgeting Magic."

This book is the culmination of my personal experience with budgeting, research, and advice from financial experts. I have seen the transformative power of budgeting in my own life and the lives of countless others. That's why I am passionate about sharing this knowledge with you.

In this book, I aim to provide a comprehensive guide to zero-based budgeting, a powerful tool that can help you achieve financial freedom and well-being. I understand that budgeting can be daunting, and that's why I've included practical tips, examples, and resources to help you get started and stay on track.

But this book is not just about budgeting. It's about transforming your relationship with money and creating a brighter financial future for yourself and your family. It's about taking control of your finances and achieving your dreams.

I want to thank you for choosing "Zero-Based Budgeting Magic." My hope is that this book will empower you to take control of your finances, achieve your goals, and create a life of abundance and prosperity. So let's dive in and start your journey towards financial well-being and success!

INTRODUCTION

Are you tired of living paycheque to paycheque, struggling with debt, or feeling like your finances are out of control? Do you want to create a solid foundation for financial success and build a brighter future for yourself and your family? If so, you're not alone. Millions of people around the world struggle with managing their finances, but the good news is that there's a powerful tool that can help you take control of your money and achieve lasting financial well-being: Zero-Based Budgeting.

"Zero-Based Budgeting Magic" is a comprehensive guide that empowers readers to transform their finances using the principles of zero-based budgeting. Whether you're just starting on your financial journey or looking to enhance your existing budgeting practices, this book provides practical tips, tools, and resources for creating and maintaining a budget that aligns with your financial goals and values.

With zero-based budgeting, you assign every pound/

euro/dollar a job, prioritising your spending based on what's most important to you. This approach provides a clear and purposeful way to manage your finances, allowing you to track your progress towards your goals and make informed decisions about your money.

In this book, you'll learn how to develop a realistic budget that reflects your unique financial situation, prioritise your expenses based on your values and goals, and track your progress towards financial freedom. You'll also explore the broader benefits of zero-based budgeting, such as improved decision-making, enhanced discipline and self-control, greater awareness and mindfulness, reduced stress, and stronger relationships.

Written in a clear and engaging style, "Zero-Based Budgeting Magic" offers practical guidance that can be applied immediately to achieve a more prosperous and fulfilling financial life. Whether you're struggling with debt, looking to build wealth, or simply seeking a more mindful approach to managing your money, this book is an indispensable resource for unlocking the magic of zero-based budgeting and achieving lasting financial well-being.

YOUR FINANCIAL WAND: ZERO-BASED BUDGETING

Imagine having a magic wand that could transform your financial life, helping you achieve your goals, pay off debt, and attain financial freedom. What if I told you that there is such a tool, and it's called zero-based budgeting? Welcome to the world of Zero-Based Budgeting Magic, where I will guide you through the process of taking control of your finances by using a budgeting method that has changed countless lives.

Zero-based budgeting (ZBB) is a powerful approach that can transform the way you manage your money, enabling you to live a life of purpose and financial clarity. It's not about cutting corners or depriving yourself; rather, it's about understanding your priorities, making mindful decisions, and working toward your financial goals with precision.

In this book, you'll learn the ins and outs of zero-based budgeting, from its origins to its practical application in daily life. I'll provide you with the tools, techniques, and tips needed to master this budgeting method and make it work for you. My aim is to help you harness the magic of zero-based budgeting so that you can enjoy the financial stability and freedom you've always dreamed of.

Now, let's embark on this enchanting journey toward financial transformation.

THE WORLD OF ZERO-BASED BUDGETING

What Is Zero-Based Budgeting?

Zero-based budgeting is a financial management approach that focuses on planning and allocating funds based on the specific needs and priorities of each budgeting period, rather than relying on the previous period's budget. In other words, every expense must be justified and approved before it is included in the budget, and the budget starts from zero each time it's created.

The primary goal of zero-based budgeting is to eliminate unnecessary expenses, promote efficiency, and allocate resources more effectively. By scrutinising every expense, you'll be able to identify areas where you can save, redirect funds towards your priorities, and gain greater control over your financial life.

The Origins Of Zero-Based Budgeting

Zero-based budgeting was first introduced by Peter A. Pyhrr in the early 1970s while working at Texas Instruments. Pyhrr's approach was later adopted by then-Governor of Georgia, Jimmy Carter, who implemented ZBB in the state's budgeting process. As Carter went on to become the 39th President of the United States, he tried to implement zero-based budgeting at the federal level, although with limited success due to the complexity of the government budgeting process.

Nonetheless, zero-based budgeting has since gained popularity in the corporate world, and more recently, in personal finance. Today, thousands of people use ZBB as a tool to gain control of their finances, pay off debt, and work toward financial independence.

Zero-Based Vs. Traditional Budgeting

Traditional budgeting methods typically involve adjusting the previous period's budget by adding or subtracting a certain percentage or amount, based on factors such as inflation or expected revenue growth. This approach may lead to inefficiencies and overspending, as it assumes that previous expenses were necessary and justified.

On the other hand, zero-based budgeting requires a thorough examination of each expense, ensuring that every pound/euro/dollar spent aligns with your financial goals and priorities. This method encourages greater financial awareness and mindfulness, making it easier to identify and eliminate unnecessary expenses.

In the next chapter, we'll explore the magic ingredients for zero-based budgeting success, laying the groundwork for your financial transformation.

THE MAGIC INGREDIENTS FOR ZERO-BASED BUDGETING SUCCESS

Setting Clear Goals And Priorities

To make the most of zero-based budgeting, it's essential to set clear financial goals and priorities. Your goals will serve as your guiding light, helping you make informed decisions about how to allocate your resources. To set effective goals, consider the following steps:

Reflect on your values and what matters most to you.

Set SMART goals (Specific, Measurable, Achievable, Relevant, and Time-bound).

Break down larger goals into smaller, manageable steps.

Regularly review and adjust your goals as needed.

By establishing clear goals and priorities, you'll be better equipped to create a budget that supports your vision for your financial future.

Establishing A Solid Financial Foundation

Before diving into zero-based budgeting, it's crucial to have a solid financial foundation in place. This includes:

Creating an emergency fund to cover unexpected expenses and provide a financial safety net.

Ensuring you have adequate insurance coverage to protect yourself and your family from unforeseen events.

Paying off high-interest debt, such as credit cards or payday loans, to reduce financial strain.

With a strong financial foundation, you'll be better prepared to make the most of zero-based budgeting and work toward your long-term financial goals.

Building A Habit Of Tracking Expenses

A key aspect of zero-based budgeting is keeping track of your expenses. By monitoring your spending, you can identify patterns and areas where you can cut back or adjust your budget. To build the habit of tracking expenses, consider these tips:

Choose a method that works for you, such as using a budgeting app, spreadsheet, or pen and paper.

Make it a daily habit to record your expenses as they occur, ensuring accuracy and consistency.

Categorise your expenses, making it easier to analyse your spending habits and make adjustments as needed.

Tracking your expenses will provide you with valuable insights into your spending habits and help you make more informed decisions about your budget.

The Power Of A Monthly Budget Meeting

One of the secrets to zero-based budgeting success is regularly reviewing and adjusting your budget. A monthly budget meeting is an opportunity for you (and your partner or family members, if applicable) to:

Review your spending from the previous month.

Assess your progress toward your financial goals.

Make adjustments to your budget based on any changes in your circumstances or priorities.

Celebrate your successes and discuss any challenges you've faced.

By holding yourself accountable and staying engaged with your budget, you'll be better positioned to achieve your financial goals and maintain control over your finances.

In the following chapter, we'll delve into the zero-based budgeting spellbook, providing you with a step-by-step guide to creating and managing your budget.

THE ZERO-BASED BUDGETING SPELLBOOK

The Budgeting Process, Step-By-Step

To create your zero-based budget, follow these steps:

Calculate your monthly income: Add up all your sources of income, including your salary, side hustles, rental income, and any other regular earnings. Use your net income (after taxes and deductions) for a more accurate budget.

List your monthly expenses: Write down all your regular expenses, including rent or mortgage, utilities, groceries, transportation, insurance, and debt payments. Don't forget to include savings, investments, and any discretionary spending.

Categorise your expenses: Organize your expenses into categories, such as housing, food, transportation, and entertainment. This will help you see where your money is going and make it easier to adjust your spending.

Assign a budget to each category: Allocate a specific amount to each expense category, ensuring that your total expenses equal your total income. This is the essence of zero-based budgeting—every pound/euro/dollar has a job.

Track your spending: As you spend throughout the month, track your expenses and compare them to your budgeted amounts. This will help you stay on track and make adjustments as needed.

Review and adjust: At the end of the month, review your spending and assess your progress towards your financial goals. Make any necessary adjustments to your budget for the next month to ensure you continue to move towards your goals.

Crafting Your Magical Budget Categories

The key to a successful zero-based budget is having well-defined categories that reflect your priorities and spending habits. Your categories should be specific enough to provide insight into your spending patterns but broad enough to be manageable. Some common categories include:

Housing (rent, mortgage, rates, insurance)

Utilities (electricity, water, fuel, internet, phone)

Food (groceries, dining out)

Transportation (fuel, public transport, car payments, insurance)

Health (insurance, medical expenses, prescriptions)

Savings (emergency fund, retirement, investments)

Debt (credit cards, student loans, personal loans)

Entertainment (movies, hobbies, sports)

Personal (clothing, grooming, gifts)

Feel free to customise your categories to suit your unique needs and preferences.

Allocating Funds To Each Category

Once you have established your categories, it's time to allocate your income to each one. Start by assigning funds to your essential expenses, such as housing, utilities, and food. Next, allocate funds to your financial goals, such as savings, debt repayment, and investments. Finally, designate funds for discretionary spending, such as entertainment and personal items.

Remember, the goal of zero-based budgeting is to ensure that every pound/euro/dollar has a purpose. Be intentional with your allocations and make sure they align with your financial priorities.

Adjusting Your Budget As Life Happens

One of the strengths of zero-based budgeting is its flexibility. As your circumstances change, you can adjust your budget to reflect your new priorities and goals. Some common reasons for adjusting your budget include:

Changes in income, such as a payrise or a job loss

Major life events, such as getting married, having a baby, or buying a home

Unexpected expenses, such as medical emergencies or car repairs

Changes in financial goals or priorities

When adjusting your budget, be mindful of your overall financial goals and ensure that any changes align with your long-term vision.

In the next chapter, we'll explore tools and techniques for automating and streamlining your zero-based budgeting experience.

AUTOMATION AND TOOLS FOR A SEAMLESS BUDGETING EXPERIENCE

Budgeting Apps And Software

In today's digital age, there are numerous apps and software programmes designed to make budgeting easier and more efficient. Some popular options for zero-based budgeting include:

You Need a Budget (YNAB): A subscription-based app that focuses on the principles of zero-based budgeting and promotes goal-setting and financial accountability.

EveryDollar: Created by personal finance guru Dave Ramsey, this app is specifically designed for zero-based budgeting, with a user-friendly interface and goal-tracking features.

Mint: A free budgeting app that offers expense tracking, bill reminders, and customisable budget categories, suitable for adapting to a zero-based budgeting approach.

Experiment with different tools to find the one that best suits your needs and preferences.

Integrating Zero-Based Budgeting With Your Financial Accounts

To streamline your zero-based budgeting process, consider integrating your budgeting tool with your financial accounts, such as your current, savings, and credit card accounts. This can help you:

Automatically import transactions, saving time and improving accuracy.

Monitor account balances in real-time, ensuring you stay on track with your budget.

Receive alerts and notifications for upcoming bills or when you're approaching the limits of your budget categories.

Many budgeting apps offer integration with financial institutions, making it easy to sync your accounts and stay up-to-date with your finances.

Harnessing The Power Of Spreadsheets

If you prefer a more hands-on approach to budgeting, spreadsheets can be a powerful and flexible tool for managing your zero-based budget. With a spreadsheet, you can:

Customise your budget categories and formulas to suit your unique needs.

Easily track and analyse your spending patterns over time.

Create visual representations of your financial progress, such as graphs and charts.

Popular spreadsheet programs like Microsoft Excel and Google Sheets offer pre-built budget templates, or you can create your own from scratch.

In the next chapter, we'll reveal some advanced zero-based budgeting techniques to help you further refine your financial strategy and accelerate your progress towards your goals.

THE SORCERER'S SECRETS: ADVANCED ZERO-BASED BUDGETING TECHNIQUES

Managing Irregular Income With Zero-Based Budgeting

If you have an irregular income, such as freelancing or seasonal work, zero-based budgeting can still be a valuable tool for managing your finances. Here are some strategies for adapting ZBB to an irregular income:

Estimate your average monthly income based on your historical earnings, and use this figure as a starting point for your budget.

Prioritise your essential expenses and financial goals, ensuring they are covered before allocating funds to discretionary spending.

Adjust your budget as needed throughout the month as your actual income becomes clearer, reallocating funds to different categories as necessary.

Saving And Investing With Zero-Based Budgeting

Zero-based budgeting can help you accelerate your savings and investment goals by ensuring all of your money is working towards your financial priorities. Consider the following tips:

Treat your savings and investments as non-negotiable expenses, allocating funds to these categories before discretionary spending.

Take advantage of employer-sponsored retirement plans, and automate your contributions to ensure consistency and benefit from any available matching contributions.

Utilise separate savings accounts or investment vehicles for different goals, such as an emergency fund, a down payment for a house, or a college savings plan.

Dealing With Debt And Paying It Off Faster

Zero-based budgeting can be a powerful tool for tackling debt and becoming debt-free faster. To use ZBB to pay off debt more quickly:

List your debts in order of priority, either by interest rate (highest to lowest) or balance (smallest to largest), depending on your preferred debt repayment strategy.

Allocate funds in your budget to make the minimum payments on all debts.

Designate any additional funds to the debt at the top of your priority list, ensuring that all your money is working to reduce your debt burden.

Preparing For Financial Emergencies

Financial emergencies, such as job loss, medical expenses, or car repairs, can derail your budget and hinder your progress towards your financial goals. Zero-based budgeting can help you build a financial safety net by:

Creating an emergency fund as a separate budget category and allocating funds to it each month until you have a sufficient cushion (typically 3-6 months of living expenses).

Regularly reviewing and updating your emergency fund goal to account for changes in your expenses or financial circumstances.

Ensuring your budget includes adequate insurance coverage to protect you and your family from unforeseen events.

In the next chapter, we'll explore the alchemy of frugal living and mindful spending, and how these principles can further enhance your zero-based budgeting experience.

THE ALCHEMY OF FRUGAL LIVING AND MINDFUL SPENDING

Embracing Frugality Without Sacrificing Joy

Frugal living doesn't have to mean deprivation or misery. In fact, it can be a powerful and enjoyable way to align your spending with your values and priorities. By embracing frugality, you can:

Discover creative ways to save money and reduce expenses.

Focus on experiences and relationships rather than material possessions.

Develop an appreciation for the simple pleasures in life.

To live frugally, look for ways to save on everyday

expenses, such as cooking at home, shopping for sales, and repurposing or repairing items instead of buying new ones. Remember, the goal is to find a balance between saving money and enjoying life.

The Art Of Mindful Spending

Mindful spending involves being intentional and deliberate with your purchases, ensuring that the money you spend aligns with your values, priorities, and goals. To practice mindful spending:

Pause before making a purchase to consider whether it's necessary and in line with your financial priorities.

Focus on quality over quantity, investing in items that will last and provide value over time.

Limit impulsive or emotional purchases by establishing a waiting period for non-essential items.

By cultivating a habit of mindful spending, you'll be better equipped to maintain control over your finances and stay on track with your zero-based budget.

Aligning Your Spending With Your Values

One of the most powerful aspects of zero-based budgeting is its ability to help you align your spending with your values. To ensure your budget reflects your priorities:

Regularly review your financial goals and priorities to ensure they are in line with your values and aspirations.

Assess your spending habits and identify areas where you can make adjustments to better support your values.

Be willing to make tough decisions and trade-offs when it comes to allocating funds in your budget, prioritising what truly matters to you.

By aligning your spending with your values, you'll be more motivated to stick to your budget and work towards your financial goals.

In the next chapter, we'll reflect on the transformative power of zero-based budgeting and provide guidance for maintaining your financial momentum as you move forward on your journey to financial freedom.

UNLEASHING THE TRANSFORMATIVE POWER OF ZERO-BASED BUDGETING

Celebrating Your Successes And Learning From Your Challenges

As you progress on your zero-based budgeting journey, it's important to take the time to celebrate your successes and acknowledge the challenges you've faced. By reflecting on your achievements and learning from your setbacks, you can:

Maintain motivation and momentum towards your financial goals.

Identify areas for improvement and adjust your

strategies as needed.

Build confidence in your ability to manage your finances effectively.

Consider sharing your successes with friends, family, or a financial accountability partner to reinforce your commitment and celebrate your victories together.

The Ripple Effects Of Financial Mastery

Mastering zero-based budgeting can have far-reaching effects on your life beyond just your finances. By gaining control over your money, you can:

Reduce stress and anxiety related to financial uncertainty.

Improve your relationships by minimising financial conflicts and fostering open communication about money matters.

Enhance your overall quality of life by aligning your spending with your values and goals.

Embrace the transformative power of zero-based budgeting, and watch as it ripples out to touch all areas of your life.

Maintaining Momentum And Staying

Committed To Your Financial Journey

As you move forward on your financial journey, remember that zero-based budgeting is not a one-time event but an ongoing process. To maintain your momentum and stay committed:

Regularly review and adjust your budget to account for changes in your circumstances or priorities.

Set new financial goals and challenges to keep yourself motivated and engaged.

Stay connected to a community of like-minded individuals who share your commitment to financial mastery, either online or in person.

By staying committed to your zero-based budgeting practice, you can continue to build a strong financial foundation and work towards a future of financial freedom and abundance.

Zero-based budgeting is a magical tool that can transform your financial life, empowering you to take control of your money and work towards your dreams. By understanding the principles, mastering the techniques, and embracing the mindset of mindful spending and frugal living, you can unlock the secrets of zero-based budgeting magic and unleash its full potential in your life.

In the next chapter we shall have a look at some real life success stories of people who have successfully incorporated zero-based budgeting into their lives.

REAL LIFE SUCCESS STORIES

There are many real-life success stories of people who have achieved financial success using zero-based budgeting. Here are just a few examples:

Dave Ramsey: Dave Ramsey is a personal finance guru who is well-known for his "baby steps" approach to financial success. One of the key steps in his programme is to use a zero-based budget to track your spending and prioritise your expenses. Ramsey's advice has helped countless individuals and families get out of debt, build wealth, and achieve financial freedom.

Lauren Greutman: Lauren Greutman is a personal finance expert and author who has written extensively about her journey from financial despair to success. Greutman and her husband used zero-based budgeting to pay off over $40,000 in debt in just two years. She now runs a successful blog and coaching business, helping others achieve their own financial goals.

Rachel Cruze: Rachel Cruze is a personal finance author, speaker, and host of the "Rachel Cruze Show." She is also the daughter of Dave Ramsey and has followed in her father's footsteps in promoting the benefits of zero-based budgeting. Cruze has helped many people overcome debt and build wealth by implementing this budgeting method.

These success stories demonstrate that zero-based budgeting can be a powerful tool for achieving financial success, no matter your income or financial situation. By being intentional with your spending and aligning your expenses with your goals and values, you can create a brighter financial future for yourself and your family.

Moreover, these success stories also demonstrate the importance of staying committed to your financial goals and being open to learning and growth. Achieving financial success is not always easy, and it requires hard work, discipline, and a willingness to make sacrifices. However, the rewards of financial freedom and well-being are well worth the effort.

If you're looking for inspiration and guidance on your own financial journey, consider seeking out the stories of others who have achieved success through zero-based budgeting and other financial strategies. You can find many resources online, including blogs, podcasts, and books, that offer practical advice and real-life examples of financial success.

Ultimately, the key to achieving financial success is to find a budgeting method that works for you and to stay committed to your financial goals. Whether you choose zero-based budgeting or another approach, remember that financial success is within your reach, and with dedication, persistence, and a growth mindset, you can create the financial future you desire.

TEMPLATES AND TOOLS FOR ZERO-BASED BUDGETING SUCCESS

To support your zero-based budgeting journey and help you stay organised and on track, you may like to research templates and tools. For example:

Zero-Based Budget Template: A customisable spreadsheet template designed to help you create and manage your zero-based budget. Your template should include sections for income, expenses, and savings goals, as well as calculations to help you track your progress and ensure that every pound/dollar/ euro is allocated.

Expense Tracking Worksheet: A worksheet for tracking your daily, weekly, and monthly expenses.

Use such a worksheet to help you monitor your spending, identify patterns, and make adjustments to your budget as needed.

Financial Goals Worksheet: A worksheet for setting short-term, mid-term, and long-term financial goals. Use your worksheet to help you clarify your financial priorities, set measurable and attainable objectives, and track your progress towards achieving your goals.

Debt Reduction Plan: A spreadsheet template designed to help you create a plan for paying off your debts. This template should include sections for listing your debts, calculating your total debt, and prioritising your repayment strategy.

Savings Goals Tracker: A worksheet for tracking your progress towards your savings goals. Use such a tracker to monitor your contributions, celebrate milestones, and stay motivated on your journey towards financial freedom.

By utilising templates and tools such as those listed above, you can streamline your zero-based budgeting process, stay organised, and maintain focus on your financial goals. Remember, the key to budgeting success is consistency and commitment – keep working on your budget, tracking your expenses, and refining your financial plan, and you'll soon discover the magic of zero-based budgeting in your life.

In addition to templates and tools mentioned,

consider exploring some popular budgeting apps and software that can help you manage your zero-based budget more efficiently. These apps often come with built-in features for tracking expenses, setting financial goals, and monitoring your progress towards financial freedom.

You Need a Budget (YNAB) – YNAB is a popular budgeting app that follows a zero-based budgeting approach, encouraging users to give every dollar a job. With YNAB, you can easily create custom budget categories, track expenses, and set savings goals. Visit their website at https://www.youneedabudget.com/.

EveryDollar – Created by Dave Ramsey, EveryDollar is a budgeting app specifically designed for zero-based budgeting. The app allows you to create your budget, allocate your income to various expense categories, and track your spending throughout the month. Check it out at https://www.everydollar.com/.

Mint – Mint is a comprehensive personal finance app that can help you create budgets, track expenses, set financial goals, and monitor your credit score. Although not explicitly designed for zero-based budgeting, it can be customised to suit this approach. Learn more at https://www.mint.com/.

Quicken – Quicken is a well-established personal finance software that offers budgeting, expense tracking, and financial planning tools. You can customise Quicken to follow a zero-based budgeting approach, and the software provides detailed reports and insights into your financial habits. Visit https://www.quicken.com/ for more information.

Tiller Money – Tiller Money is a budgeting tool that automatically updates Google Sheets or Microsoft Excel with your financial data, allowing you to create and manage your budget in a familiar spreadsheet environment. With customisable templates, Tiller Money can be adapted to zero-based budgeting. Check out their website at https://www.tillerhq.com/.

Keep in mind that each of these apps and software options may have different pricing structures and features. Be sure to research and compare them to find the one that best suits your needs and preferences. By leveraging technology, you can streamline your zero-based budgeting process and stay on track towards achieving your financial goals.

As you continue to practice zero-based budgeting and utilise the various tools, templates, and resources available, it's essential to stay engaged with your personal finance journey. One way to keep learning and growing in your financial understanding is by connecting with others who share similar goals and interests.

Here are some ways to connect with like-minded

individuals and continue learning about zero-based budgeting and personal finance:

Online Forums and Communities – Join online forums, social media groups, or Reddit communities focused on personal finance and budgeting. Some popular forums include the r/personalfinance and r/ynab subreddits, as well as the Mr. Money Mustache Forums.

Local Meetups and Workshops – Attend local personal finance meetups, workshops, or seminars in your area to connect with others interested in budgeting, saving, and investing. Check out websites like Meetup.com to find events near you.

Book Clubs – Start or join a personal finance book club with friends, family, or colleagues to discuss books like "Zero-Based Budgeting Magic" and other personal finance literature. This can help deepen your understanding and provide an opportunity to learn from the experiences of others.

Online Courses – Enroll in online courses or webinars on personal finance topics to further your education and connect with other learners. Websites like Coursera, Udemy, and edX offer a variety of personal finance courses, often taught by experts in the field.

Financial Coaching – If you're looking for personalised guidance and support, consider working with a financial coach. These professionals can help you create a customised financial plan, navigate challenges, and stay accountable to your goals.

By actively engaging with others interested in personal finance and zero-based budgeting, you can continue to learn, grow, and stay motivated on your journey to financial freedom. The magic of zero-based budgeting is a continuous process that requires dedication, adaptability, and a commitment to lifelong learning. With the right mindset, tools, and support, you can achieve lasting financial success and enjoy the benefits of a stable and prosperous financial future.

A LIFETIME OF FINANCIAL EMPOWERMENT

As you begin to incorporate "Zero-Based Budgeting Magic" into your life, consider how the journey you've embarked upon is one that will continue to evolve and grow with you. By consistently practicing zero-based budgeting, mindful spending, and frugal living, you are forging a path towards a lifetime of financial empowerment and stability.

Keep these key thoughts in mind as you continue to hone your budgeting skills:

Zero-based budgeting is an ongoing process that requires commitment, discipline, and adaptability.

Regularly review and adjust your budget to align with your changing financial goals and circumstances.

Embrace mindful spending and frugal living to make the most of your financial resources and maintain control over your money.

Celebrate your successes and learn from your challenges as you progress on your journey to financial freedom.

The magic of zero-based budgeting lies in its ability to transform not only your finances but also your mindset, priorities, and overall well-being. Armed with the knowledge and tools at your disposal, you'll be well-prepared to face your financial future with confidence and determination.

As you forge ahead on your path to financial mastery, remember that the most powerful tool at your disposal is your own commitment to growth and improvement. Stay focused, stay motivated, and continue to unleash the transformative power of zero-based budgeting in your life. With persistence and dedication, you'll soon discover that the true magic of zero-based budgeting lies within you.

SHARING THE MAGIC OF ZERO-BASED BUDGETING

As you experience the benefits of zero-based budgeting in your own life, consider sharing this powerful financial tool with others. By helping friends, family, and colleagues discover the magic of zero-based budgeting, you can create a ripple effect that promotes financial empowerment and stability throughout your community.

Here are some ways to share the magic of zero-based budgeting with others:

Lead by example: Demonstrate the effectiveness of zero-based budgeting through your own financial successes and commitment to mindful spending and frugal living.

Share your story: Speak openly about your experiences with zero-based budgeting, including the challenges you've faced, the lessons you've learned, and the successes you've achieved.

Offer guidance: Offer to help others create their own zero-based budgets, sharing the techniques and strategies you've learned from this book and your personal experience.

Organise workshops or study groups: Bring together individuals interested in learning about zero-based budgeting, and facilitate discussions, workshops, or study sessions to explore the concepts and practices together.

Encourage others to read "Zero-Based Budgeting Magic": Recommend this book to friends, family, and colleagues who may benefit from its insights and guidance.

By sharing the magic of zero-based budgeting with others, you can help create a world where financial empowerment and stability are accessible to everyone. So go forth, spread the word, and let the magic of zero-based budgeting touch the lives of those around you.

MOVING ON

It's important to periodically evaluate your financial situation and make any necessary adjustments. Life is constantly changing, and your budget should reflect those changes to ensure you stay on track with your financial goals. Here are some tips for keeping your zero-based budget up-to-date and effective:

Regularly review your budget: Set aside time each month, quarter, or year to review your budget and make any necessary adjustments. This will help you stay proactive in managing your finances and ensure that your budget remains aligned with your current financial situation and goals.

Monitor your spending: Keep a close eye on your expenses and track them regularly to ensure you're sticking to your budget. If you notice any areas where you're consistently overspending, take the time to reevaluate your budget and make adjustments as needed.

Update your financial goals: As you achieve your short-term financial goals or your priorities change, update your budget to reflect your new objectives. This will help you stay focused on what's important to you and maintain motivation as you work towards your long-term financial goals.

Adjust for life changes: Major life events, such as a new job, marriage, or the birth of a child, can have a significant impact on your financial situation. When these changes occur, reevaluate your budget and make any necessary adjustments to ensure it remains relevant and effective.

Seek feedback and support: Don't be afraid to ask for help or advice from trusted friends, family members, or financial professionals. They can provide valuable insights, share their experiences, and offer guidance as you navigate the complexities of budgeting and personal finance.

The real advantage of zero-based budgeting lies in its adaptability and responsiveness to your unique financial situation. By staying engaged with your budget, making adjustments as needed, and seeking support when necessary, you can continue to harness the power of zero-based budgeting and create a strong foundation for lasting financial success.

In addition to following these tips for maintaining and updating your zero-based budget, consider expanding your personal finance knowledge in other areas as well. By broadening your understanding of various financial topics, you can make more informed decisions and enhance your overall financial well-being.

Some areas to explore include:

Investing: Learn about different investment options, such as stocks, bonds, mutual funds, and real estate, as well as strategies for building a diversified investment portfolio that aligns with your risk tolerance and financial goals.

Retirement planning: Understand the importance of saving for retirement and explore various retirement accounts. Learn about strategies for maximising your retirement savings and ensuring a comfortable retirement.

Tax planning: Familiarise yourself with the basics of income taxes, deductions, and credits. Learn about strategies for minimising your tax liability and maximising your refund, as well as how to properly file your tax return.

Insurance: Understand the role of insurance in protecting your financial well-being, and explore various types of insurance, such as life, health, home, and car insurance. Learn about factors to consider when selecting insurance policies and coverage levels.

Estate planning: Learn about the importance of estate planning and the various tools and strategies available, such as wills, trusts, and power of attorney documents. Understand how to plan for the future and protect your assets and loved ones.

Credit management: Understand the importance of maintaining a good credit score and learn strategies for building and improving your credit. Familiarise yourself with the factors that impact your credit score and how to monitor your credit report for accuracy.

By expanding your financial knowledge and understanding beyond zero-based budgeting, you can develop a comprehensive approach to managing your personal finances. This holistic perspective will empower you to make smarter financial decisions and pave the way for a more secure and prosperous future.

As your financial situation evolves and your understanding of personal finance deepens, it's important to maintain a growth mindset and embrace continuous improvement. Applying the principles of zero-based budgeting and other financial best practices will become more natural over time, but it's crucial to remain curious and open to learning.

Below are some strategies for fostering a growth mindset and staying engaged with your personal finance journey:

Stay informed: Keep up-to-date with the latest

financial news, trends, and developments by regularly reading personal finance blogs, listening to podcasts, and following financial experts on social media.

Reflect on your progress: Periodically take a step back and assess your financial growth, celebrating your accomplishments and identifying areas where you can improve. Use this reflection as an opportunity to refine your financial goals and strategies.

Embrace setbacks and learn from mistakes: Understand that setbacks are a natural part of the learning process, and use them as opportunities to grow and improve. Analyse your financial missteps to identify the lessons they hold, and apply these insights to future decisions.

Seek mentorship: Connect with individuals who have achieved financial success or share your financial goals, and learn from their experiences, insights, and advice. A mentor can offer valuable guidance, support, and motivation throughout your personal finance journey.

Challenge yourself: Set ambitious financial goals that push you beyond your comfort zone and inspire you to grow. By continually challenging yourself, you'll stay motivated, build resilience, and develop the skills and knowledge needed to achieve your long-term financial objectives.

By adopting a growth mindset and remaining committed to lifelong learning, you'll be better equipped to navigate the complexities of personal finance and adapt to the ever-changing financial landscape. With persistence, dedication, and a focus on continuous improvement, you can unlock the full potential of zero-based budgeting and create a solid foundation for lasting financial success.

In summary, the magic of zero-based budgeting lies in its ability to provide clarity, control, and a sense of purpose to your financial life. By consistently applying the principles of zero-based budgeting and utilising the various tools, resources, and strategies discussed throughout this book, you can create a personalised financial plan that aligns with your unique goals and priorities.

The journey to financial freedom is not a linear path, but rather a dynamic process that requires adaptability, resilience, and a commitment to lifelong learning. As you grow and evolve, so too should your financial plan. By maintaining a growth mindset, staying engaged with your personal finances, and seeking support when needed, you can navigate the challenges and opportunities that lie ahead with confidence and determination.

Zero-based budgeting is not just about numbers, spreadsheets, or calculations; it's about empowering yourself to take control of your financial destiny and creating a brighter future for yourself and your loved ones. So, embrace the power of zero-based budgeting and embark on a transformative journey towards financial freedom and lasting success.

Bear in mind these points:

Zero-based budgeting is a proactive and purpose-driven approach to personal finance that assigns all of your money a job, ensuring that your income is allocated towards your financial goals and priorities.

To create a zero-based budget, start by identifying your income, expenses, and financial goals, and then allocate your income to cover these items in a way that aligns with your priorities.

Regularly review and adjust your budget to reflect changes in your financial situation, priorities, and goals.

Utilise tools, templates, and resources to streamline your zero-based budgeting process and stay organised.

Connect with others who share your financial goals and interests to foster a growth mindset, stay motivated, and continue learning.

With these principles, you are well-equipped to harness the magic of zero-based budgeting and embark on a journey towards financial freedom and prosperity.

ADDITIONAL BENEFITS OF ZERO-BASED BUDGETING

The benefits of zero-based budgeting extend beyond your financial life. By practicing this budgeting method, you'll also develop valuable skills and habits that can positively impact other areas of your life.

Here are some additional benefits of zero-based budgeting:

Improved decision-making: Zero-based budgeting encourages you to think critically about your priorities and make intentional choices about how you allocate your resources. This mindful approach to decision-making can translate to other aspects of your life, helping you make better choices in your career, relationships, and personal development.

Enhanced discipline and self-control: By

consistently sticking to your budget and holding yourself accountable for your spending, you'll develop a greater sense of discipline and self-control. These qualities can help you achieve success in other areas of your life, such as maintaining a healthy lifestyle, pursuing personal goals, or staying organised.

Greater awareness and mindfulness: Zero-based budgeting promotes a deeper understanding of your financial habits, needs, and values. This heightened awareness can foster a greater sense of mindfulness in your daily life, helping you live more intentionally and find greater satisfaction in your experiences.

Reduced stress and increased peace of mind: By taking control of your financial situation and working towards your financial goals, you can experience reduced stress and anxiety related to money. This peace of mind can have a positive impact on your overall well-being, leading to a healthier, happier, and more fulfilling life.

Stronger relationships: When you have a clear understanding of your financial situation and goals, you can communicate more effectively with your partner or family members about money matters. This open and honest communication can help strengthen your relationships and promote a sense of shared purpose and collaboration.

BROADER BENEFITS OF ZERO-BASED BUDGETING

The magic of zero-based budgeting is not only about transforming your financial life but also about fostering personal growth and enrichment. By embracing the principles of zero-based budgeting, you'll cultivate valuable skills, habits, and perspectives that can have a lasting, positive impact on all areas of your life.

Now that you're well-versed in the principles of zero-based budgeting and understand the broader benefits of this approach, it's time to put this knowledge into action. As you begin your journey towards financial freedom, keep the following steps in mind to ensure a smooth and successful transition:

Commit to the process: Embrace zero-based budgeting wholeheartedly and make a commitment to stick with it, even when challenges arise. Remember that it may take time to fully adapt to this new way of managing your finances, so be patient with yourself and trust the process.

Set clear financial goals: Establish specific, measurable, achievable, relevant, and time-bound (SMART) financial goals that align with your priorities and values. These goals will serve as the foundation of your zero-based budget and provide a clear roadmap for your financial journey.

Develop a realistic budget: Use the principles of zero-based budgeting to create a budget that accurately reflects your income, expenses, and financial goals. Be honest with yourself about your spending habits and prioritise your expenses based on your unique needs and priorities.

Track your progress: Regularly monitor your spending and compare it to your budget to ensure you're staying on track. Adjust your budget as needed to accommodate changes in your financial situation or goals.

Learn and grow: Stay engaged with your personal finance journey by continually seeking out new information, resources, and support. Be open to learning from your experiences, both positive and negative, and apply these insights to your financial decisions moving forward.

By following these steps and maintaining a growth mindset, you can unlock the full potential of zero-based budgeting and achieve lasting financial success. Zero-based budgeting empowers you to take control of your financial destiny, create a brighter future for yourself and your loved ones, and foster personal growth and enrichment in all areas of your life. Embrace the journey, stay focused on your goals, and enjoy the rewards that come with financial freedom and well-being.

ALTERNATIVES TO ZERO-BASED BUDGETING

While zero-based budgeting can be a powerful tool for managing your finances, it's not the only approach available. Here are a few alternative budgeting methods you may want to research and consider:

Envelope budgeting: With this approach, you use cash envelopes to allocate your funds to different categories of expenses, such as groceries, fuel, or entertainment. Once the envelope is empty, you stop spending in that category until the next budgeting period. This method can be helpful for those who struggle with overspending or find it challenging to track their expenses digitally.

50/30/20 budgeting: This approach involves dividing your after-tax income into three categories:

50% for needs, such as housing and utilities, 30% for wants, such as entertainment and dining out, and 20% for savings and debt repayment. This method can be useful for those who want a simple, straightforward budgeting approach.

Priority-based budgeting: With this approach, you prioritize your spending based on what's most important to you. You identify your top financial goals, such as paying off debt, building an emergency fund, or saving for a down payment on a home, and allocate your funds accordingly. This method can be helpful for those who want to align their spending with their values and goals.

Value-based budgeting: This approach involves identifying your core values and using them as a guide for your spending. You allocate your funds to activities and purchases that align with your values, such as travel, education, or supporting a cause you care about. This method can be useful for those who want to make sure their spending reflects their personal beliefs and priorities.

Ultimately, the best budgeting method for you will depend on your individual financial situation, goals, and values. It may take some trial and error to find the approach that works best for you. However, by experimenting with different methods and staying committed to your financial goals, you can achieve greater financial well-being and build a brighter future for yourself and your loved ones.

PARTING WORDS

Zero-based budgeting is a powerful tool that can transform your financial life, but it's up to you to take action and make it work for you.

As you embark on your zero-based budgeting journey, don't forget to remain flexible, open to learning, and committed to your goals. Keep in mind that achieving financial success takes time and effort, but with persistence, dedication, and a growth mindset, you can create the financial future you desire.

Some parting words of wisdom to keep in mind as you work towards your financial goals are:

Prioritise your needs over your wants: It's important to distinguish between essential expenses, such as housing, food, and utilities, and discretionary spending, such as entertainment or luxury purchases. By prioritising your needs over your wants, you can ensure that your budget aligns with your long-term financial goals.

Build an emergency fund: Life is full of unexpected

events, and it's important to be prepared for emergencies. Build an emergency fund that covers at least three to six months of your living expenses, so you have a safety net in case of job loss, illness, or other unforeseen circumstances.

Avoid debt: High-interest debt can be a major setback to your financial goals, so it's important to avoid it whenever possible. If you have debt, focus on paying it off as quickly as possible, and avoid taking on new debt unless it's necessary and manageable.

Invest for the future: Don't just save your money; invest it wisely to build wealth over time. Explore various investment options and strategies, such as retirement accounts, stocks, bonds, and mutual funds, and seek guidance from a financial professional if needed.

Celebrate your progress: Don't forget to celebrate your financial milestones along the way, no matter how small they may seem. Celebrating your progress can help motivate you to continue working towards your goals and provide a sense of accomplishment and satisfaction.

With these principles in mind, you can continue to make progress towards your financial goals and achieve the financial freedom and prosperity you deserve. And always remember that your financial journey is unique to you, and there is no one-size-fits-all approach to achieving financial success. Keep an open mind and be willing to adapt your approach as your financial situation and goals evolve.

Moreover, do not forget to enjoy the process and find joy in the journey. While financial freedom is undoubtedly a worthwhile goal, it's also essential to find happiness and fulfillment in other areas of your life. Strive for balance, and know that your financial well-being is just one aspect of your overall well-being.

FURTHER READING AND RESOURCES

To continue your journey towards financial mastery and delve deeper into the world of personal finance, consider exploring the following books and resources:

Books:

The Total Money Makeover by Dave Ramsey – This classic personal finance book offers a step-by-step plan for achieving financial freedom, including guidance on budgeting, debt reduction, and building wealth.

Your Money or Your Life by Vicki Robin and Joe Dominguez – This groundbreaking book explores the relationship between money, work, and fulfillment, and provides a nine-step program for transforming your financial life.

Rich Dad Poor Dad by Robert Kiyosaki – This best-selling book offers valuable insights into personal finance, investing, and wealth-building through the contrasting lessons learned from the author's "rich dad" and "poor dad."

I Will Teach You to Be Rich by Ramit Sethi – This practical guide to personal finance covers everything from budgeting and saving to investing and negotiating, with a focus on automation and behavioral change.

Websites and Blogs:

The Simple Dollar (thesimpledollar.com) – A personal finance blog offering practical advice on saving money, investing, and making smart financial decisions.

Mr. Money Mustache (mrmoneymustache.com) – A blog focused on frugality, investing, and financial independence, with a wealth of resources and a supportive community.

Get Rich Slowly (getrichslowly.org) – A personal finance blog that offers advice on budgeting, saving, investing, and other aspects of personal finance, with an emphasis on slow and steady progress towards financial goals.

Online Courses and Workshops:

Financial Peace University (financialpeace.com) – A nine-week course created by Dave Ramsey that covers topics such as budgeting, debt reduction, and investing, with a focus on building financial peace and freedom.

The YNAB (You Need a Budget) Workshops (youneedabudget.com) – Free online workshops that provide guidance on budgeting, debt reduction, and financial goal-setting, with a focus on the YNAB budgeting app and methodology.

Podcasts:

The Dave Ramsey Show (daveramsey.com/show) – A daily podcast featuring financial advice, listener calls, and expert interviews, with a focus on budgeting, debt reduction, and wealth-building.

ChooseFI (choosefi.com) – A podcast dedicated to exploring the world of financial independence, with episodes covering topics such as budgeting, investing, and frugal living.

By continuing to expand your financial knowledge and exploring additional resources, you'll be better equipped to navigate the ever-changing landscape of personal finance and stay on the path towards financial empowerment and freedom.

ABOUT THE AUTHOR

Sinéad Hoben

Sinéad Hoben is a teacher and writer with a passion for helping individuals and families achieve financial success and stability. She graduated with a BA(Hons) in English and a Postgraduate Certificate in Education in English with Drama and Media from the University of Ulster. Her academic background and experience in education have provided her with a strong foundation in communication and teaching.

Since having a family, Sinéad has developed a particular interest in saving and budgeting. She understands the unique challenges and opportunities that come with managing household finances and has dedicated herself to finding practical solutions to help families make the most of their money. Through her research and firsthand experience, Sinéad has gained extensive knowledge of budgeting techniques, including the cash stuffing system, zero-based budgeting, the 50:30:20 approach and other budgeting methods which she shares in her writing. Her writing and editing skills have allowed her to effectively communicate complex financial concepts in an accessible and engaging manner, making her a valuable resource for those looking to improve their financial well-being.

Through her writing and educational endeavours, Sinéad strives to empower individuals and families to take control of their finances, develop healthy money habits, and work towards their financial goals with confidence.

ACKNOWLEDGEMENT

I would like to extend my gratitude to the many individuals who contributed to the creation of this book. Without their insights, support, and encouragement, this guide to zero-based budgeting would not have been possible.

First and foremost, I am grateful to the countless financial experts, educators, and personal finance enthusiasts who have dedicated their time and energy to advancing the field of budgeting and financial planning. Their work has laid the foundation for the principles and techniques explored in this book.

I would also like to thank the many readers and practitioners of zero-based budgeting who have shared their stories, struggles, and successes. Your experiences have helped to shape the content and structure of this book, ensuring that it remains relevant, accessible, and practical for a wide range of audiences.

Finally, I extend my deepest appreciation to my

family, who have provided unwavering support and encouragement throughout the writing process. Your belief in the power of zero-based budgeting and the potential impact of this book on the lives of its readers has been a constant source of inspiration.

I look forward to witnessing the positive impact this book will have on the financial lives of its readers, and I remain committed to supporting the ongoing journey towards financial empowerment and freedom for all.

BOOKS BY THIS AUTHOR

Cash Stuffing Magic: Transform Your Household Budgeting With The Envelope System

Are you tired of living paycheque to paycheque and feeling stressed about your finances? Cash Stuffing Magic: Transform Your Household Budgeting with the Envelope System is the practical guide you need to take control of your finances and achieve financial success.

Written by teacher and mother of four, Sinéad Hoben, this book shares her passion for helping individuals and families transform their financial lives with the envelope system. With easy-to-follow steps, real-life success stories, and additional resources, Cash Stuffing Magic will help you create a budget, stick to it, and achieve your financial goals. Plus, learn how to use technology to complement the cash stuffing system, deal with unexpected expenses and emergencies, build wealth and plan for retirement, and develop the mindset and behaviour changes necessary for lasting financial success.

Don't let money stress you out - start your journey to financial freedom with Cash Stuffing Magic.

9 798390 971949